KINGFISHER
READERS

level

W9-BPS-866

Chimpanzees

Claire Llewellyn

KINGFISHER
NEW YORK

KINGFISHER
LONDON & NEW YORK

Copyright © Macmillan Publishers International Ltd 2015
Published in the United States by Kingfisher,
175 Fifth Ave., New York, NY 10010
Kingfisher is an imprint of Macmillan Children's Books, London.
All rights reserved.

Distributed in the U.S. and Canada by Macmillan,
175 Fifth Ave., New York, NY 10010

Library of Congress Cataloging-in-Publication data
has been applied for.

Series editor: Thea Feldman
Literacy consultant: Ellie Costa, Bank Street College, New York

978-0-7534-7225-5 (HB)
978-0-7534-7226-2 (PB)

Kingfisher books are avilable for special promotions
and premiums. For details contact: Special Markets
Department, Macmillan, 175 Fifth Ave.,
New York, NY 10010.

For more information, please visit
www.kingfisherbooks.com

Printed in China

9 8 7 6 5 4 3 2 1
1TR/0615/WKT/UG/105MA

Picture credits
The Publisher would like to thank the following for permission to reproduce their material.
Top = t; Bottom = b; Center = c; Left = l; Right = r
Cover Shutterstock/Eric Gevaert; Pages 4-5, 8, 13 Shutterstock/Sergey Uryadnikov; 5t Shutterstock/Kjersti
Joergensen; 6 Shutterstock/Steffan Foerster; 7 Shutterstock/EBFoto; 9t Alamy/Duncan McKay; 10 Naturepl/
Anup Shah; 11t Shutterstock/Kletr; 11b, 22, 25 FLPA/Frans Lanting; 12, 24 FLPA/Minden Pictures/Cyril
Ruoso; 14 Shutterstock/Sam DCruz; 15 Naturepl/Suzi Eszterhas; 16 Shutterstock/tratong; 17t Shutterstock/
Colette3; 17b Shutterstock/apple2499; 18 Getty/Dr Clive Bromhall; 19, 26 Alamy/Steve Bloom Images;
20 Getty/Minden Pictures/Cyril Ruoso; 21t Shutterstock/Patryk Kosmider; 21b Shutterstock/Eric Gevaert;
23 FLPA/Minden Pictures/Ingo Arndt; 27 FLPA/Imagebroker/Konrad Wothe; 28 Shutterstock/Ben Carlson;
29 Shutterstock/Lorimer Images; 30 Alamy/Martin Harvey; 31 Alamy/Duncan McKay.

Contents

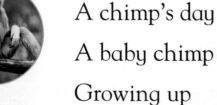

Meet the chimpanzee

Chimpanzees are only found in the wild in Africa.

They are also called chimps.

Chimps live together in groups.

Kinds of chimps

There are two kinds of chimps.

This chimp is called
a common chimp.

This chimp is a
bonobo chimp.

Trees, please!

Chimps live in **rainforests**, woods, and other places in Africa that have trees.

Trees are very important to chimps.

Chimps find food in trees.

They sleep in tree branches at night.

On the move

Chimps swing from tree to tree by gripping branches with their long, strong fingers and toes.

Chimps lean on
the **knuckles** of
their hands
when they walk
on all fours.

Life in a group

A chimp group can have
15 to 150 chimps!

Each group has adult and young chimps.

An adult male leads each group.

He will fight other chimps to protect his group and their home.

Let's eat!

Chimps eat all the different parts of plants.

They eat plant stems, leaves, flowers, and fruit.

Chimps also hunt and eat monkeys, pigs, insects, and other animals.

Animal kinds

Chimps are **mammals**.

There are many kinds of mammals.

Chimps are mammals called **apes**.

All these animals are apes.

Apes do not have tails and they can hold things in their fingers and toes.

Using tools

This chimp
uses a
flat stone
to smash
the shells
of nuts.

These chimps catch **termites** by
poking a stick into a termite mound.

Termites crawl onto the stick
and the chimps eat them!

Communicating

Chimps call out to each other in the forest, where lots of leaves can make it hard to see each other.

Chimps make faces to communicate.

A chimp shows its top teeth when it is nervous.

Chimps also touch each other to show affection.

21

A chimp's day

A chimp wakes up
at dawn.

It calls to others
and finds food.

At midday, chimps
rest and **groom**
each other.

At sunset, chimps make nests
in the treetops, where
they will spend the night.

A baby chimp

A baby chimp needs
its mother's milk for the
first five years of its life.

When it is about six months old,
a chimp begins to play with
other chimps in the group.

Growing up

A male chimp begins to spend a lot of time with other male chimps when he turns eight years old.

He helps protect his entire group.

At age eight, a female chimp
learns how to be a mother
by watching her own mother
with her younger **siblings**.

Chimps in danger

Chimps are **endangered** animals.

They lose their homes when people cut down trees and use their land.

Some people eat chimps,
and some sell them as pets.

Protecting chimps

Some scientists study chimps
in the wild to learn about them
and how we can protect them.

Some countries turn their forests into **national parks**.

Tourists pay to visit the parks.

The money helps protect chimps.

Glossary

apes animals that do not have tails and that can hold things in their fingers and toes

endangered a kind of living thing that is at risk of dying out

groom to clean an animal's fur

knuckles the places where your fingers bend

mammals animals with fur that feed their milk to their babies

national parks land that is protected by the government

rainforest a forest that is hot all year and gets more than 6 feet (1.8 meters) of rain a year

siblings brothers or sisters

termites one of many kinds of insects that live together